Sports Illustrated KIDS

SIDE BY SIDE

HOCKEY STARS

Comparing Pro Hockey's Greatest Players

BY SHANE FREDERICK

CAPSTONE PRESS
a capstone imprint

SIDE-BY-SIDE HOCKEY STARS:
Comparing Pro Hockey's Greatest Players

The Penguins' Sidney Crosby and the Capitals' Alex Ovechkin entered the league together in 2005 and have been two of the most exciting players since. Years ago, Wayne Gretzky and Mario Lemieux drew close comparisons. Before that, it was Gordie Howe and Maurice Richard.

But what if the best players of today could take on the best players of the past? Would Steven Stamkos be able to outscore Gordie Howe in a game? In a season? Would P.K. Subban put up more points than Raymond Bourque? Now it's time to place those players from different eras side by side and see who really stands out. Decide for yourself who would win in these superstar matchups.

*All stats are through the 2013–14 regular season.

Sports Illustrated Kids Side-By-Side Sports are published by Capstone Press, 1710 Roe Crest Drive, North Mankato, Minnesota 56003
www.capstonepub.com

Sports Illustrated Kids is a trademark of Time Inc. Used with permission.

Printed in the United States of America in Stevens Point, Wisconsin.
032014   008092WZF14

TABLE OF CONTENTS

SIDNEY
CROSBY

NICKNAME: Sid the Kid
HEIGHT: 5 feet, 11 inches (180 cm)
WEIGHT: 200 pounds (91 kg)
YEARS ACTIVE: 2005–present*
TEAM: Penguins
ALL-STAR GAMES: 1
FIRST TEAM NHL ALL-STAR: 2 times
STANLEY CUP CHAMPIONSHIPS: 1
HART MEMORIAL TROPHIES (MVP): 1
-Led NHL in points twice
-Led NHL in goals once

Games	Goals	Assists	Points	PIM
550	274	495	769	463

*Stats are through the 2013–14 regular season.

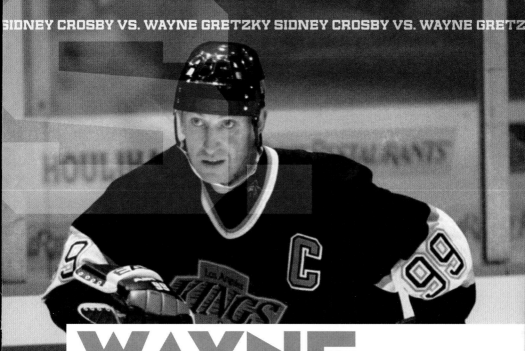

WAYNE GRETZKY

NICKNAME: The Great One
HEIGHT: 6 feet (183 cm)
WEIGHT: 185 pounds (84 kg)
YEARS ACTIVE: 1979–1999
TEAMS: Oilers, Kings, Blues, Rangers
ALL-STAR GAMES: 18
FIRST TEAM NHL ALL-STAR: 8 times
STANLEY CUP CHAMPIONSHIPS: 4
HART MEMORIAL TROPHIES (MVP): 9
CONN SMYTHE TROPHIES (PLAYOFF MVP): 2
-Led NHL in scoring 11 times
-NHL's all-time leader in goals, assists, and points
-Holds single-season records for goals, assists, and points
-Entered the Hall of Fame in 1999

Games	Goals	Assists	Points	PIM
1,487	894	1,963	2,857	577

SIDNEY CROSBY

> "He's dynamite. He's the best player I've seen since Mario [Lemieux]. He's that good."
> —*NHL great Wayne Gretzky*

> "I've won the Stanley Cup, won gold medals. Getting Sidney Crosby was the happiest day of my life." —*Penguins executive Craig Patrick*

Sidney Crosby's hardly a kid anymore, but he accomplished so much at a young age that the nickname "Sid the Kid" stuck with him. Before the age of 20, Crosby had already scored 200 points. He was the youngest player in history to reach that milestone. He also

was the youngest player at the time to be named an NHL team captain. Crosby went a step further and became the youngest player to captain a team to a Stanley Cup championship. He was just 21 years old when he was handed the historic trophy for the first time.

In 2006–07 Crosby amassed 120 points, becoming the first teenager to lead the league in scoring. He was also the youngest scoring champion ever in a North American team sport. In his first six seasons, Crosby won a Stanley Cup, an MVP, and a scoring title, despite being limited by injuries.

WAYNE GRETZKY

When you consider Wayne Gretzky's many records, which is the most impressive? Is it the 2,857 points? The 894 goals? The 51-game point-scoring streak? Gretzky once scored 50 goals in just 39 games, 11 games faster than the previous mark. If you took away every goal he scored during his career, his assist total would still make him the NHL's all-

time leading scorer. As Hall of Famer Marcel Dionne once said, "There's a record book for Wayne and one for everybody else in the league."

No other player in NHL history has scored 200 or more points in a season, and Gretzky did it four times. Those seemingly untouchable records are why the NHL—not just the teams "The Great One" played for—retired his famous number 99.

> "There's only one way to stop Wayne Gretzky, and that's to lock him in the dressing room."
> —*NHL great Gordie Howe*

> "Gretzky sees a picture out there that no one else sees. It's difficult to describe because I've never seen the game he's looking at."
> —*Former Bruins general manager Harry Sinden*

JONATHAN
TOEWS

NICKNAME: Captain Serious
HEIGHT: 6 feet, 2 inches (188 cm)
WEIGHT: 208 pounds (94 kg)
YEARS ACTIVE: 2007–present*
TEAM: Blackhawks
ALL-STAR GAMES: 2
STANLEY CUP CHAMPIONSHIPS: 2
CONN SMYTHE TROPHIES (PLAYOFF MVP): 1
FRANK J. SELKE TROPHIES (TOP DEFENSIVE FORWARD): 1

Games	Goals	Assists	Points	PIM
484	195	245	440	257

*Stats are through the 2013–14 regular season.

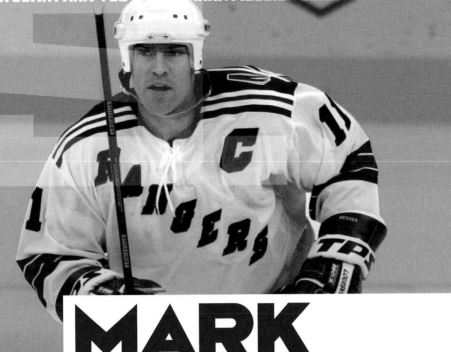

MARK MESSIER

NICKNAME: Moose
HEIGHT: 6 feet, 1 inch (185 cm)
WEIGHT: 210 pounds (95 kg)
YEARS ACTIVE: 1979–2004
TEAMS: Oilers, Rangers, Canucks
ALL-STAR GAMES: 15
FIRST TEAM NHL ALL-STAR: 4 times
STANLEY CUP CHAMPIONSHIPS: 6
HART MEMORIAL TROPHIES (MVP): 2
CONN SMYTHE TROPHIES (PLAYOFF MVP): 1
-Ranks second all-time in points and third in assists
-Entered the Hall of Fame in 2007

Games	Goals	Assists	Points	PIM
1756	694	1193	1887	1910

JONATHAN TOEWS

It didn't take the Chicago Blackhawks long to figure out they had something special in Jonathan Toews. As a rookie, Toews scored a point in each of his first 10 NHL games, the third-longest point streak to start a career. It also didn't take Chicago long to realize it had a real leader in Toews.

During his second season, the 19-year-old was named team captain, an important position and high honor in the sport of hockey. In his third year, Toews led the Blackhawks to their first Stanley Cup championship in 49 years. Playing like a seasoned veteran, he scored 29 points in 22 playoff games. The Blackhawks won the title again three years later. Toews joined Wayne Gretzky as the only players in NHL history to captain two Cup-winning teams before age 25.

"He's such a special person, to start off with. The way he handles himself. The pressure this team had going into this year, he kind of put that all on his shoulders and carried us. So you can't explain. He's just a special kid."

—Blackhawks teammate Andrew Ladd

"He's one of those once-in-a-generation type of players as far as I'm concerned."

—Blackhawks president John McDonough

During the 1993 Eastern Conference finals, Mark Messier's New York Rangers faced elimination in the series against the New Jersey Devils. But the captain promised a Rangers win in Game 6. With his team trailing 2-1 in the third period, Messier made his guarantee come true, scoring three goals for a 4-2 victory. The Rangers won Game 7 and went on to defeat the Vancouver Canucks in seven games for their first championship in 54 years. Messier became the first NHL player to captain two different teams to championships. He had won with the Edmonton Oilers five times, including once after the great Wayne Gretzky had been traded away.

"The measure of Mark's game is not in goals and assists. The statistic he cares about is number of Stanley Cups won."
—NHL great Wayne Gretzky

"Messier only has three speeds—fast, faster, and fastest." —Hockey Hall of Famer Emile Francis

EVGENI
MALKIN

NICKNAME: Geno
HEIGHT: 6 feet, 3 inches (191 cm)
WEIGHT: 195 pounds (89 kg)
YEARS ACTIVE: 2006–present*
TEAM: Penguins
ALL-STAR GAMES: 3
FIRST TEAM NHL ALL-STAR: 3 times
STANLEY CUP CHAMPIONSHIPS: 1
HART MEMORIAL TROPHIES (MVP): 1
CONN SMYTHE TROPHIES (PLAYOFF MVP): 1
**AWARDED 2007 CALDER MEMORIAL TROPHY
  (ROOKIE OF THE YEAR)**
-*Led NHL in scoring twice*

Games	Goals	Assists	Points	PIM
518	240	392	632	524

*Stats are through the 2013–14 regular season.

MARIO
LEMIEUX

NICKNAME: Super Mario
HEIGHT: 6 feet, 4 inches (193 cm)
WEIGHT: 230 pounds (104 kg)
YEARS ACTIVE: 1984–1997, 2000–2006
TEAM: Penguins
ALL-STAR GAMES: 10
FIRST TEAM NHL ALL-STAR: 5 times
STANLEY CUP CHAMPIONSHIPS: 2
HART MEMORIAL TROPHIES (MVP): 3
CONN SMYTHE TROPHIES (PLAYOFF MVP): 2
AWARDED 1985 CALDER MEMORIAL TROPHY (ROOKIE OF THE YEAR)
-*Led NHL in scoring six times*
-*Entered the Hall of Fame in 1997*

Games	Goals	Assists	Points	PIM
915	690	1,033	1,723	834

EVGENI MALKIN

As a 20-year-old rookie in 2006–07, Evgeni Malkin did not come into the NHL quietly. He scored a goal in his first game for the Pittsburgh Penguins. He then proceeded to score at least one goal in the next five games as well. Statisticians combed the record books and had to go all the way back to 1917—89 years—to find the last time a rookie had accomplished the feat. Malkin had eight goals and 11 points in that stretch, and the Penguins won all six of those games.

Malkin has proved as valuable as teammate Sidney Crosby. He has led the NHL in scoring and has won an MVP. After leading Pittsburgh to a Stanley Cup, he became the first Russian-born player to be named playoff MVP.

"He's as close to Mario [Lemieux] in terms of size and what he can do with the puck as we've seen in a while."

—Former Penguins teammate Mark Recchi

"He told us before the playoffs started that he was going to lead us to the Stanley Cup. That kid is an amazing competitor and amazing player. He has a lot of character and a lot of heart." —Former Penguins teammate Bill Guerin

Look at a list of the top-scoring seasons in NHL history, and Wayne Gretzky's name is everywhere. But take a closer look, and you'll see another name pop up often. Of the 13 highest-scoring seasons, Gretzky has nine, but Mario Lemieux has the other four, including a 199-point season in 1988–89. On New Year's Eve of that season, Lemieux became the first NHL player to score five goals in five different situations (even strength, power play, short-handed, penalty shot, and empty net).

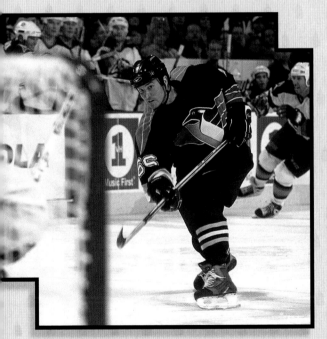

Lemieux ranks seventh all-time in points, but injury and illness kept him from climbing higher. He retired in 1997 despite winning his sixth scoring title that year. He returned in 2000 and played five more seasons, becoming one of just three players to return to the ice after being inducted into the Hockey Hall of Fame.

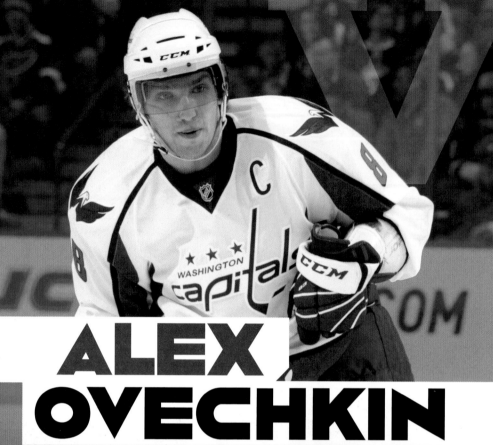

ALEX OVECHKIN

NICKNAME: Alexander the Great
HEIGHT: 6 feet, 3 inches (191 cm)
WEIGHT: 230 pounds (104 kg)
YEARS ACTIVE: 2005–present*
TEAM: Capitals
ALL-STAR GAMES: 4
FIRST TEAM NHL ALL-STAR: 6 times
HART MEMORIAL TROPHIES (MVP): 3
**AWARDED 2006 CALDER MEMORIAL TROPHY
   (ROOKIE OF THE YEAR)**
-Led NHL in scoring once
-Led NHL in goals four times

Games	Goals	Assists	Points	PIM
679	422	392	814	456

*Stats are through the 2013–14 regular season.

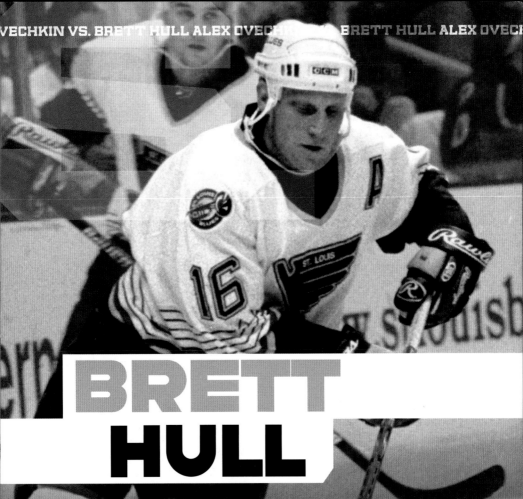

BRETT
HULL

NICKNAME: The Golden Brett
HEIGHT: 5 feet, 11 inches (180 cm)
WEIGHT: 203 pounds (92 kg)
YEARS ACTIVE: 1986–2006
TEAMS: Flames, Blues, Stars, Red Wings, Coyotes
ALL-STAR GAMES: 8
FIRST TEAM NHL ALL-STAR: 3 times
STANLEY CUP CHAMPIONSHIPS: 2
HART MEMORIAL TROPHIES (MVP): 1
-Led NHL in goals three times
-Ranks third all-time in career goals
-Entered the Hall of Fame in 2009

Games	Goals	Assists	Points	PIM
1,269	741	650	1,391	458

There are many NHL defenders who figured they had Alexander Ovechkin stopped. They pushed him to the outside. They knocked him to the ice. The next thing those opponents saw, however, was the puck in the back of their net. They'd find Ovechkin celebrating from whatever position they had left him in, even if that position was on his back with his skates in the air.

Against the Phoenix Coyotes in 2006, Ovechkin had fallen to the ice and was sliding away from the goal. Yet he reached over his head and backhanded the puck into the net—a play so unusual it was called "The Goal." In 2010 against the New York Rangers, Ovechkin had a defenseman draped all over him and could only get one hand on his stick. Still, he found the strength to get off a shot for the goal. In his first nine seasons, Ovechkin ranked among the NHL's top five goal scorers eight times.

"On the bench, we can feel it—we can feel how he just grabs a hold of the game and goes after it. He charges down the ice, and every time he has the puck you think he's going to score."
—Capitals teammate Brooks Laich

"He gets the puck, goes hard. And when he doesn't have the puck, he's forechecking—bang, crash. He's come to us as close to perfect as there is." —Former Capitals coach Glen Hanlon

BRETT HULL

It was the third overtime of Game 6 of the 1999 Stanley Cup Finals, and Brett Hull found himself in front of the goal. He fired the puck into the net, and the celebration began for the Dallas Stars. Hull had sealed the championship.

Like his father, Bobby Hull, he was a natural when it came to scoring goals. He ranks third all-time in goals and second all-time in power-play goals. From 1989 to 1992, Brett Hull had a three-season stretch in which he racked up 228 goals for the St. Louis Blues. Only Wayne Gretzky had a better three-year run, scoring 250 goals between 1981 and 1984. Hull's 86 goals during the 1990–91 season marked the last time an NHL player has touched the 80-goal threshold.

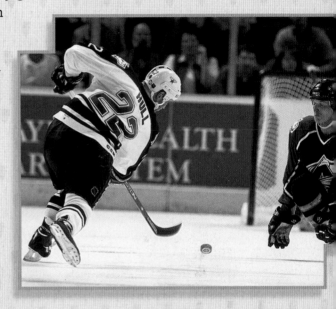

"Being able to make a boyhood dream come true is one thing, but to have a kid come along and thrill his dad like Brett Hull has thrilled me over his career is too much for one guy to handle."

—Hockey Hall of Famer Bobby Hull, Brett's father

"You think Brett, you think pure goal-scorer. One of the best I have ever seen."

—Former NHL player Jeremy Roenick

STEVEN
STAMKOS

NICKNAME: Stammer
HEIGHT: 6 feet, 1 inch (185 cm)
WEIGHT: 191 pounds (87 kg)
YEARS ACTIVE: 2008–present*
TEAM: Lightning
ALL-STAR GAMES: 2
-Led NHL in goals twice

Games	Goals	Assists	Points	PIM
410	233	193	426	267

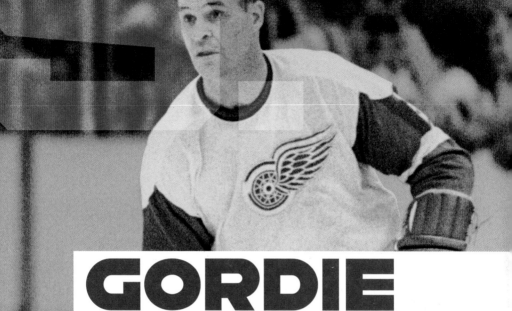

GORDIE HOWE

NICKNAME: Mr. Hockey
HEIGHT: 6 feet (183 cm)
WEIGHT: 205 pounds (93 kg)
YEARS ACTIVE: 1946–1971, 1980
TEAMS: Red Wings, Whalers
ALL-STAR GAMES: 23
FIRST TEAM NHL ALL-STAR: 12 times
STANLEY CUP CHAMPIONSHIPS: 4
HART MEMORIAL TROPHIES (MVP): 6
-Led NHL in scoring six times
-Led NHL in goals five times and assists three times
-Ranks third all-time in scoring and second in goals
-Entered the Hall of Fame in 1972

Games	Goals	Assists	Points	PIM
1767	801	1049	1850	1685

"He's kinda claimed that spot that was reserved for [Brendan] Shanahan, Ovechkin, and myself. I watch him on TV and I go, 'Boy, does that ever look familiar.'" —*NHL great Brett Hull*

"If hockey were golf, they would break down his swing and everyone would try to copy it."
—*Lightning teammate Martin St. Louis*

Steven Stamkos is the master of the one-timer. Leave the Tampa Bay Lightning forward open on the faceoff dot of the left circle, and he's downright deadly. His shot from the left circle was once called "hockey's biggest weapon." On a one-timer, a player doesn't catch a pass—he simply shoots the puck as it comes to him. If the timing's just right, the puck meets the sweet spot of the blade at the moment the stick swings over the ice. Stamkos has racked up goals from that spot, as well as other places on the ice.

Stamkos scored 51 goals in his second season, 2010–11. The next season, he increased that to 60, a milestone reached by just one other player since 1996. Stamkos' total included five winning goals in overtime, a single-season NHL record.

GORDIE HOWE

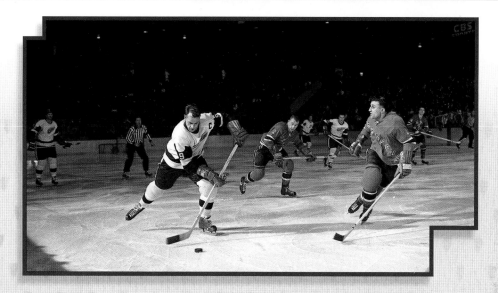

Before there was Wayne Gretzky, there was Gordie Howe. "Mr. Hockey," as he came to be known, set the records Gretzky would eventually pass. Few others were able to get anywhere near his numbers. Howe compiled 1,850 points in the NHL, mostly during his 25-year career with the Detroit Red Wings. He added another 508 points after coming out of retirement and playing six seasons in the World Hockey Association (WHA).

In his final season with the Hartford Whalers, the WHA had merged with the NHL. Howe was back in the NHL, skating on a team with his sons Mark and Marty at the age of 51. He played in 80 games that season, scoring 15 goals and assisting on 26 others.

"I could never compare myself to him. He's Mr. Hockey." —*NHL great Mark Messier*

"The only way to stop Howe is to crowd him, stop him before he gets started, but nobody wants to crowd Gordie. Nobody even wants to get near him." —*Former Red Wings defenseman Kent Douglas*

MARTIN
BRODEUR

NICKNAME: The Door
HEIGHT: 6 feet, 2 inches (188 cm)
WEIGHT: 220 pounds (100 kg)
YEARS ACTIVE: 1991–present*
TEAM: Devils
ALL-STAR GAMES: 9
FIRST TEAM NHL ALL-STAR: 4 times
STANLEY CUP CHAMPIONSHIPS: 3
VEZINA TROPHIES (TOP GOALIE): 4
WILLIAM M. JENNINGS TROPHIES (LOWEST GOALS AGAINST): 5
**AWARDED 1994 CALDER MEMORIAL TROPHY
   (ROOKIE OF THE YEAR)**
-All-time leader in goalie wins and shutouts
-Led NHL in shutouts five times

Games	Wins	Shutouts	Save%	GAA
1,259	688	124	.912	2.24

*Stats are through the 2013–14 regular season.

DOMINIK HASEK

NICKNAME: The Dominator
HEIGHT: 6 feet, 1 inch (185 cm)
WEIGHT: 166 pounds (73 kg)
YEARS ACTIVE: 1990–2008
TEAMS: Sabres, Red Wings
ALL-STAR GAMES: 6
FIRST TEAM NHL ALL-STAR: 6 times
STANLEY CUP CHAMPIONSHIPS: 2
HART MEMORIAL TROPHIES (MVP): 2
VEZINA TROPHIES (TOP GOALIE): 6
WILLIAM M. JENNINGS TROPHIES (LOWEST GOALS AGAINST): 3
-All-time leader in save percentage
-Led NHL in save percentage six times and shutouts four times

Games	Wins	Shutouts	Save%	GAA
735	389	81	.922	2.20

MARTIN BRODEUR

Martin Brodeur doesn't have to wait until he retires to be considered among the best goaltenders of all time. He may already be at the top of the list. Playing more than two decades for the New Jersey Devils, he has set new standards for goalies. He may have set the bar too high for anyone else to reach.

Brodeur's record for career victories is 100 wins higher than the total for the next goalie on the list. He has enough shutouts on his resume to fill nearly a season and a half of NHL games. In 2003 Brodeur led the Devils to the Stanley Cup championship for the third time. Along the way, he shut out the Anaheim Ducks three times, including the Cup-clinching Game 7, when he stopped all 24 shots he faced.

"[W]hen Marty Brodeur finally leaves the NHL, with him will go the most unique, exciting goaltending style of all time."
—*Former Devils goaltender and broadcaster Chico Resch*

"There's Marty after the second period, having his Sprite and half a bagel, working on a shutout, and he's talking and joking with the guys in the room. Then he'll go out and stop 10 shots in the third. There's just this calmness about him." —*Former Devils teammate Sheldon Souray*

DOMINIK HASEK

They called him "Dominator," and in the late 1990s, few goaltenders dominated the net like Dominik Hasek. In 1997, while playing for the Buffalo Sabres, Hasek stopped 93 percent of the pucks that came his way and allowed just 2.27 goals per game. Voters had little choice but to award him the Hart Trophy as the NHL's most valuable player. It was the first time since 1962 that a goalie had received the award.

A year later, Hasek was even better. Facing more shots and making more saves than any other goalie in the league, he upped his save percentage to .932. He lowered his goals-against average to 2.09 by shutting out 13 opponents. Naturally, the league gave him the Hart Trophy again.

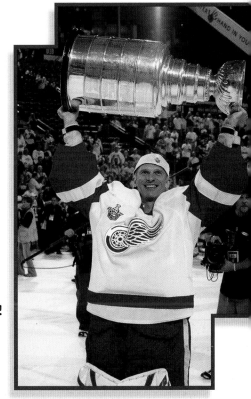

"Like all of the really great ones, the special athletes, Dom saw the play develop before it happened. ... His ability to slow down the speed of the puck was extraordinary."

—*Former NHL goalie and broadcaster Darren Pang*

"They say I am unorthodox, I flop around the ice like some kind of fish. I say, who cares as long as I stop the puck?"

—*Dominik Hasek*

JONATHAN QUICK

NICKNAME: Quickie
HEIGHT: 6 feet, 1 inch (185 cm)
WEIGHT: 218 pounds (99 kg)
YEARS ACTIVE: 2007–present*
TEAM: Kings
ALL-STAR GAMES: 1
STANLEY CUP CHAMPIONSHIPS: 1
CONN SMYTHE TROPHIES (PLAYOFF MVP): 1
-*Led NHL in shutouts once*

Games	Wins	Shutouts	Save%	GAA
335	176	31	.915	2.28

*Stats are through the 2013–14 regular season.

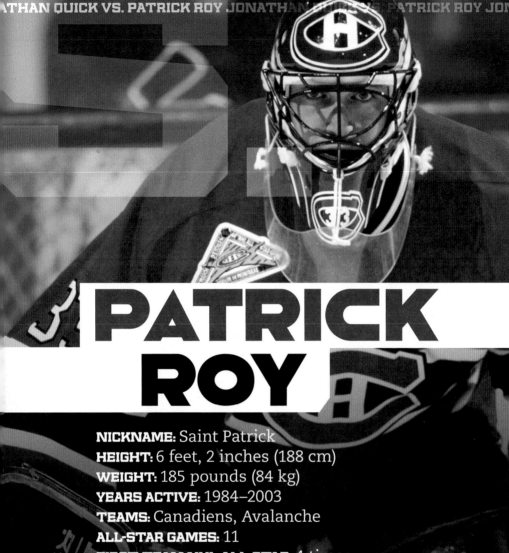

PATRICK ROY

NICKNAME: Saint Patrick
HEIGHT: 6 feet, 2 inches (188 cm)
WEIGHT: 185 pounds (84 kg)
YEARS ACTIVE: 1984–2003
TEAMS: Canadiens, Avalanche
ALL-STAR GAMES: 11
FIRST TEAM NHL ALL-STAR: 4 times
STANLEY CUP CHAMPIONSHIPS: 4
VEZINA TROPHIES (TOP GOALIE): 3
WILLIAM M. JENNINGS TROPHIES (LOWEST GOALS AGAINST): 5
CONN SMYTHE TROPHIES (PLAYOFF MVP): 3
-Led NHL in save percentage four times and shutouts three times
-Entered the Hall of Fame in 2006

Games	Wins	Shutouts	Save%	GAA
1,029	551	66	.910	2.54

The Los Angeles Kings snuck into the 2012 Stanley Cup playoffs as a number eight seed. Experts predicted they would be eliminated quickly by the Western Conference's top seed, the Vancouver Canucks. But the Kings were the ones doing things quickly—because they had Jonathan Quick. Quick put together one of the best playoff goaltending performances in NHL history. The Kings knocked off the Canucks and three other teams to win their first Stanley Cup. Quick stopped an amazing 94.6 percent of opponents' shots. He allowed only 1.41 goals per game, the lowest average since the Montreal Canadiens' Jacques Plante had 1.35 in 1960. In the Finals Quick out-dueled the New Jersey Devils' Martin Brodeur, allowing just six goals in six games. Quick was named MVP of the playoffs.

"He's a battler. He never quits on pucks. Saves you think he can't make he makes every game. We're not here without him. We're not even in the conversation." —*Kings teammate Drew Doughty*

"He's one of the best goaltenders I've ever seen. He's also one of the best teammates ever because he's such a selfless guy. I'll make a mistake, it'll end up in our net, and he won't glare or say anything except, 'I shoulda had it.' Love the guy." —*Kings teammate Willie Mitchell*

When he was a 20-year-old rookie in 1986, Patrick Roy led the Montreal Canadiens to their 23rd Stanley Cup championship. He became the youngest player to be named the Conn Smythe Trophy winner as playoff MVP. But Roy had to do more to get compared to Montreal greats Ken Dryden, Jacques Plante, and George Hainsworth.

In 1993 Roy went 16-4 in the playoffs. He stopped nearly 93 percent of opponents' shots and allowed just 2.13 goals per game. In the Finals, he held the great Wayne Gretzky to just two goals in five games. He also won three overtime games against the Los Angeles Kings, as the Canadiens won their 24th title. Roy was traded to the Colorado Avalanche in the middle of the 1995–96 season, and he promptly led that team to the first of two championships.

"There's no doubt with the style he plays and success he's had, people mirror him. You can try to mirror someone's style, but it's what's inside that makes the player. With Patty, it's determination and will."

—*Former NHL goaltender Mike Vernon*

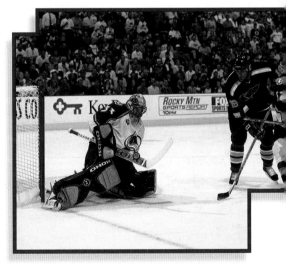

"I can't think of a weak spot. So you just shoot enough and hope he makes a mistake on one." —*NHL player Jarome Iginla*

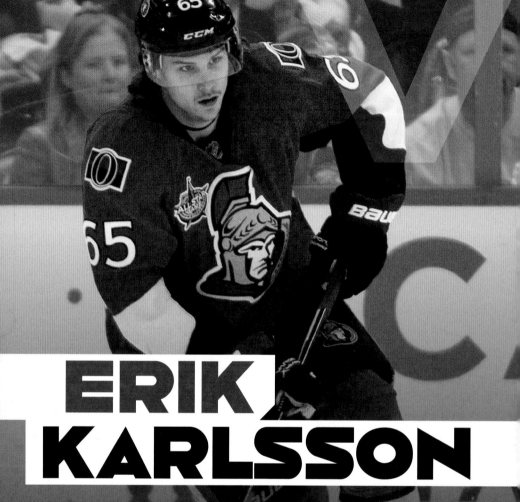

ERIK KARLSSON

NICKNAME: Karl
HEIGHT: 6 feet (183 cm)
WEIGHT: 180 pounds (82 kg)
YEARS ACTIVE: 2009–present*
TEAM: Senators
ALL-STAR GAMES: 2
FIRST TEAM NHL ALL-STAR: 1 time
NORRIS MEMORIAL TROPHIES (TOP DEFENSEMAN): 1
-Ranked third in NHL in assists in 2011–12

Games	Goals	Assists	Points	PIM	+/-
315	63	174	237	160	-27

BOBBY
ORR

NICKNAME: Number 4
HEIGHT: 6 feet (183 cm)
WEIGHT: 197 pounds (89 kg)
YEARS ACTIVE: 1967–1979
TEAMS: Bruins, Blackhawks
ALL-STAR GAMES: 7
FIRST TEAM NHL ALL-STAR: 8 times
STANLEY CUP CHAMPIONSHIPS: 2
AWARDED 1967 CALDER MEMORIAL TROPHY
   (ROOKIE OF THE YEAR)
HART MEMORIAL TROPHIES (MVP): 3
NORRIS MEMORIAL TROPHIES (TOP DEFENSEMAN): 8
CONN SMYTHE TROPHIES (PLAYOFF MVP): 2
-*Led NHL in scoring twice and assists five times*
-*Entered the Hall of Fame in 1979*

Games	Goals	Assists	Points	PIM	+/-

On February 13, 2012, Erik Karlsson—the reigning Norris Trophy winner—got his Achilles tendon cut by the skate of an opposing player. The injury was a devastating blow to the Ottawa Senators, who had hopes of making the playoffs. Karlsson was declared out for the season, with recovery expected to take four to six months. Just 10 weeks later, however, Karlsson returned to the ice. Three games remained in the regular season, and he was determined to help the Senators hold their playoff spot. He succeeded, assisting on four goals in those games.

Small but speedy, Karlsson has become one of the most offensively skilled defensemen in hockey. When he won the Norris Memorial Trophy at age 21, he was the youngest player to be named the NHL's best defenseman since Bobby Orr won it at age 20.

"He's special. He has the determination and willpower to do anything."

—*Senators teammate Craig Anderson*

"I recognized right away how good he is. He has all the tools, all the potential. One of the things that has surprised me is how quickly he's developed. Sometimes it takes a little longer, but it seems he's ahead of the pattern."

—*Former Senators teammate Sergei Gonchar*

BOBBY ORR

Before Bobby Orr, there was a reason defensemen were called blueliners. When their teams had the puck, they rarely strayed from the blue line, and their job simply was to defend. But the talented Orr had other ideas. During overtime of Game 4 of the 1970 Stanley Cup Finals, Orr carried the puck deep into the offensive zone. He passed to teammate Derek Sanderson and skated across to the net. Sanderson gave the puck back to Orr, who tapped it behind St. Louis Blues goalie Glenn Hall. Then he dove across the crease like Superman to celebrate the championship-clinching goal. It was the Bruins' first title in almost 30 years.

Orr shattered scoring records for defensemen throughout his career and remains the only blueliner to win an NHL scoring championship. He accomplished the feat twice, including a 135-point performance in 1974–75.

> "He doesn't beat you because he's Bobby Orr; he beats you because he is the best."
>
> —*Longtime NHL coach and executive Glen Sather*

> "He could thread a needle with the puck, shoot it like a bullet or float it soft. Orr was the only player who could dictate the tempo of the game, speed it up or slow it down. He could see the whole ice the way a spectator sees it from above. He's the best player I've seen.
>
> —*Former Bruins teammate Eddie Johnston*

P.K. SUBBAN

NICKNAME: Subbanator
HEIGHT: 6 feet (183 cm)
WEIGHT: 206 pounds (93 kg)
YEARS ACTIVE: 2009–present*
TEAM: Canadiens
FIRST TEAM NHL ALL-STAR: 1 time
NORRIS MEMORIAL TROPHIES (TOP DEFENSEMAN): 1

Games	Goals	Assists	Points	PIM	+/-
284	42	125	167	282	+18

RAYMOND
BOURQUE

NICKNAME: Bubba
HEIGHT: 5 feet, 11 inches (180 cm)
WEIGHT: 219 pounds (99 kg)
YEARS ACTIVE: 1979–2001
TEAMS: Bruins, Avalanche
ALL-STAR GAMES: 19
FIRST TEAM NHL ALL-STAR: 13 times
STANLEY CUP CHAMPIONSHIPS: 1
AWARDED THE 1980 CALDER MEMORIAL TROPHY
   (ROOKIE OF THE YEAR)
NORRIS MEMORIAL TROPHIES (TOP DEFENSEMAN): 5
-NHL's all-time top-scoring defenseman
-Entered the Hall of Fame in 2004

Games	Goals	Assists	Points	PIM	+/-
1,612	410	1,169	1,579	1,141	+528

For a young player joining a storied franchise, it might be difficult to make a big splash. The Montreal Canadiens franchise is more than 100 years old. The team has 24 Stanley Cup championships, and 51 of its former players are in the Hockey Hall of Fame. But Pernell Karl "P.K." Subban was still able to turn heads in his first season with Montreal. Subban

scored three goals during a game in March 2011—something that no Canadiens defenseman had done during his rookie season. Two seasons later, after tying for the league lead in scoring for defensemen, Subban was given the Norris Memorial Trophy as the best blueliner in the NHL.

"If you take P.K. Subban [for the Olympic team] you're going to win a gold medal."

—*NHL great Wayne Gretzky*

"He's just starting to scratch the surface of what his potential is."

—*Canadiens teammate Josh Gorges*

RAYMOND BOURQUE

If Bobby Orr opened the door for defensemen to do more offensively, Raymond Bourque skated right through it. As a rookie for the Boston Bruins in 1979–80, Bourque began filling the skates Orr left behind four years earlier. He compiled 65 points, including 17 goals, his first season. He continued to score, putting up 20 goals or more in nine seasons. He scored 90 points or more four times, including a career-high 96 (with 31 goals) in 1983–84. He never won an Art Ross trophy as the league's top scorer or had a 100-point season as Orr did. But his long career and consistency made him the NHL's all-time leading scorer among defensemen. Bourque earned trips to 19 All-Star Game appearances. Only Gordie Howe played in more All-Star Games (21).

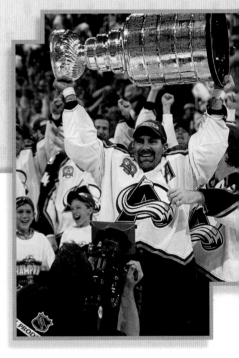

"There was no one in the game who was more committed to playing well each and every shift. There was no cutting corners for Raymond. He held so much respect for the game."

—*Former Bruins teammate Don Sweeney*

"What's amazing is that a lot of people who claim to know so much about the league really don't realize how great of a player Ray Bourque was and how he made others around him better." —*Avalanche teammate Joe Sakic*

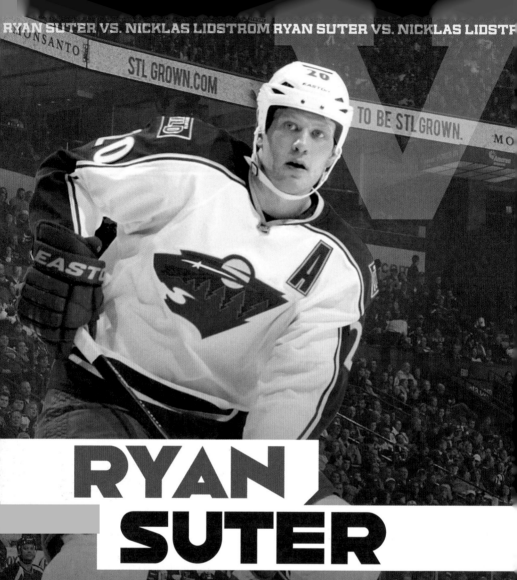

RYAN SUTER

NICKNAME: Suts

HEIGHT: 6 feet, 1 inch (185 cm)

WEIGHT: 198 pounds (90 kg)

YEARS ACTIVE: 2005–present*

TEAMS: Predators, Wild

ALL-STAR GAMES: 1

FIRST TEAM NHL ALL-STAR: 1 time

Games	Goals	Assists	Points	PIM	+/-
672	50	263	313	454	+60

NICKLAS LIDSTROM

NICKNAME: The Perfect Human
HEIGHT: 6 feet, 1 inch (185 cm)
WEIGHT: 192 pounds (87 kg)
YEARS ACTIVE: 1991–2012
TEAM: Red Wings
ALL-STAR GAMES: 11
FIRST TEAM NHL ALL-STAR: 10 times
STANLEY CUP CHAMPIONSHIPS: 4
NORRIS MEMORIAL TROPHIES (TOP DEFENSEMAN): 7
CONN SMYTHE TROPHIES (PLAYOFF MVP): 1
-Ranks sixth all-time in scoring among defensemen

Games	Goals	Assists	Points	PIM	+/-
1,564	264	878	1,142	514	+450

RYAN SUTER

Hockey is played in shifts to give the players time to rest. In a 60-minute regulation game, the top defensemen get around 25 minutes of time on the ice. But in the first game of the 2013 Stanley Cup playoffs, it seemed as if the Minnesota Wild's Ryan Suter was always on the ice. The Wild lost to the Chicago Blackhawks 2-1 at 16:35 of overtime, meaning the game lasted 76 minutes, 35 seconds. Suter was on the ice for more than 41 of those minutes. In 2013 he led the NHL in time on ice. Among defensemen, he was second in assists and third in points.

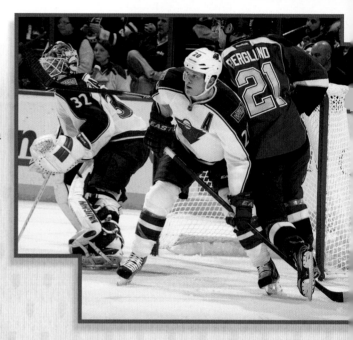

"I don't know how he does it. He gets to the bench after a two-minute shift and he's not even breathing heavy."

—*Wild teammate Zach Parise*

"He plays the score of the game as well as anybody in the league. He was the most underrated player in the whole [2010] Olympics. He was more competitive against fierce competition than anybody in the tournament." —*NHL coach Ken Hitchcock*

NICKLAS LIDSTROM

Nicklas Lidstrom's teammates can't recall him ever having a bad game. His coaches can't think of a time he made a bad mistake. For 20 seasons, the Detroit Red Wings defenseman simply did everything right. Lidstrom led the Red Wings to the playoffs every year of his career, including four championship runs.

Born and trained in Sweden, Lidstrom made history in 2002 by becoming the first European player to win the Conn Smythe Trophy. In 2008 he became the first European player to captain a Stanley Cup winner. He finished his career plus-450, meaning while he was on the ice, his team scored 450 more goals than it gave up. He also stayed out of the penalty box, averaging just 25 penalty minutes a season.

"We call him The Perfect Human. And there's a reason for it. Whatever he does, he seems to do perfectly, so I think that's a pretty good nickname."

—*Former Red Wings teammate Niklas Kronwall*

"If you could rattle him, you might get him off his game. Except I've never seen him rattled. He anticipates defensively the way [Wayne] Gretzky and [Mario] Lemieux anticipated offensively."

—*NHL coach Dave Tippett*

Sidney Crosby vs. Wayne Gretzky:

Sidney Crosby might be the best player of his generation, but Wayne Gretzky is the greatest player of all time. Crosby will likely never match Gretzky's records—and probably no one else will either. The pick: Gretzky.

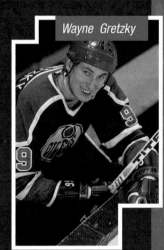
Wayne Gretzky

Jonathan Toews vs. Mark Messier:

There's a reason the NHL's leadership award is named after Mark Messier. He'll go down as one of the greatest leaders the NHL has ever seen. Jonathan Toews? He's moving up the list and fast. But his two titles are still four short of Moose's six. The pick: Messier.

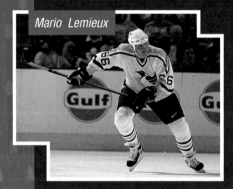
Mario Lemieux

Evgeni Malkin vs. Mario Lemieux:

When you see the 6-foot, 3-inch (191-cm) Evgeni Malkin in a Penguins uniform, it's hard not to think about another big Pittsburgh center—Mario Lemieux. Super Mario won two Stanley Cups and now owns the team, while Malkin has one title. The pick: Lemieux.

Alex Ovechkin vs. Brett Hull:

When it comes to pure goal scoring, Alex Ovechkin and Brett Hull are two of the all-time greats. Hull led the league in goal scoring three times. Ovechkin has done it four times and there could be more in his future. It's a close call. The pick: Ovechkin.

Steven Stamkos vs. Gordie Howe:

Steven Stamkos is one of the best goal scorers of his generation, but Mr. Hockey got his nickname for a reason.

Martin Brodeur vs. Dominik Hasek:

Goaltenders don't win the Hart Trophy as MVP very often, and Hasek earned it twice. But when all is said and done, Martin Brodeur might have statistics that, like Gretzky's scoring numbers, will never be touched. The pick: Brodeur.

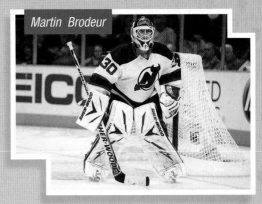

Martin Brodeur

Jonathan Quick vs. Patrick Roy:

Jonathan Quick had an extraordinary performance to lead the Los Angeles Kings to the Stanley Cup championship in 2012. To catch Patrick Roy, he'll have to do it three more times. The pick: Roy.

Erik Karlsson vs. Bobby Orr:

Early in his career, Erik Karlsson is putting up offensive numbers that have drawn comparisons to Bobby Orr. There seems to be little doubt that he's a special player. But it would be tough to take him over one of the best defensemen of all time. The pick: Orr.

P.K. Subban vs. Raymond Bourque:

P.K. Subban has some big skates to fill playing for the Montreal Canadiens. He's handling himself well and is building a great career. But there's still a long, long way to go to catch Raymond Bourque, the NHL's top-scoring defenseman. The pick: Bourque.

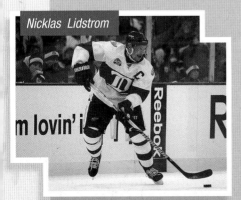

Nicklas Lidstrom

Ryan Suter vs. Nicklas Lidstrom:

Ryan Suter, it seems, rarely leaves the ice for the Minnesota Wild. He's one of the best defensemen currently playing in the NHL. But he's not The Perfect Human, although championships could change that. The pick: Lidstrom.

Critical Thinking Using the Common Core

1. With which two teams has Mark Messier won Stanley Cup Championships? (Key Ideas and Details)

2. Reread pages 24–31. If you had to pick one of the four goaltenders to protect your net, which goalie would you choose? Why? Support your choice with information from the text. (Key Ideas and Details)

3. Look at the choices the author made on pages 44 and 45 of the Coach's Call section. Do you agree with his picks? Why or why not? Support your choices with information from this book, as well as from other books or online sources. (Integration of Knowledge and Ideas)

Quotation Sources

www.jockbio.com, 6a, 6b, 14a, 18a; Zeisler, Laurel. Historical Dictionary of Ice Hockey. Lanham, Md.: Scarecrow Press, Inc., 2013, 7a; Dryden, Steve (ed). *The Top 100 NHL Players of All Time.* The Hockey News. Toronto: 1997 Transcontinental Sports Publications, 7b; www.espn.go.com, 10a, 10b, 19a, 39b, 43a; http://sportsillustrated.cnn.com, 11a, 15b, 22a, 22b, 23a, 23b, 26b, 30a, 30b, 31a, 31b, 43b; www.sportsquotation.blogspot.com, 11b; www.nhl.com, 14b, 42a; www.orlandosentinel.com, 15a; www.ovechkinfans.com, 18b; www.philly.com, 19b; www.martinbrodeur30.com, 26a; www.usatoday.com, 27a; www.nytimes.com, 27b; www.theglobeandmail.com, 34a, 34b, 38b; http://bobbyorr.net, 35a, 35b; www.fannation.com, 38a; www.legendsofhockey.net, 39a; www.startribune.com, 42b

Read More

Frederick, Shane. *The Ultimate Collection of Pro Hockey Records.* Sports Illustrated Kids. North Mankato, Minn.: Capstone Press, 2013.

Gitlin, Marty. *The Stanley Cup: All About Pro Hockey's Biggest Event.* Sports Illustrated Kids. North Mankato, Minn.: Capstone Press, 2013.

Morrison, Jessica. *Wayne Gretzky: Greatness on Ice.* New York: Crabtree Pub., 2011.

Shuker, Ronnie, ed. *The Biggest of Everything in Hockey.* The Hockey News. Toronto: Transcontinental, 2013.

Internet Sites

FactHound offers a safe, fun way to find Internet sites related to this book. All of the sites on FactHound have been researched by our staff.

Here's all you do:

Visit *www.facthound.com*

Type in this code: 9781476561660

 **Super-cool stuff!** Check out projects, games and lots more at **www.capstonekids.com**

Index

Library of Congress Cataloging-in-Publication Data
Frederick, Shane.
  Side-by-side hockey stars : comparing pro hockey's greatest players / by Shane Frederick.
      pages cm.—(Sports Illustrated kids. Side-by-side sports)
  Includes bibliographical references and index.
  Summary: "Compares the greatest pro hockey players in history"—Provided by publisher.
  ISBN 978-1-4765-6166-0 (library binding)
  ISBN 978-1-4765-6171-4 (paperback)
  1. Hockey players—Biography—Juvenile literature. 2. Hockey players—Rating of—Juvenile literature. 3. National Hockey League—Juvenile literature. I. Title.
    GV848.5.A1F743 2015
    796.9620922—dc23   2014007825

Editorial Credits
Anthony Wacholtz, editor; Ted Williams, designer; Eric Gohl, media researcher; Gene Bentdahl, production specialist ·

Photo Credits
Getty Images: Bruce Bennett Studios, 21, Focus On Sport, 33, NY Daily News/Charles Hoff, 23; Newscom: Icon SMI/Bill Vaughan, 9, Icon SMI/Jeanine Leech, 34, Icon SMI/Robert Beck, 29, Icon SMI/Shelly Castellano, 11, UPI Photo Service, 17, UPI Photo Service/Jason Szenes, 5, ZUMA Press/Matthew Manor, 32; Sports Illustrated: Bob Rosato, 22, Damian Strohmeyer, 18, 20, 24, 26, 36, 38, David E. Klutho, cover (top), 4, 6, 8, 10, 12, 13, 14, 15, 16, 19, 25, 27, 28, 31, 39, 40, 41, 42, 44 (bottom), 45 (all), John Biever, 43, John D. Hanlon, 35, John W. McDonough, 30, Tony Triolo, cover (bottom), 7, 37, 44 (top)

Design Elements: Shutterstock